11/13/00
$14.00
I

11/00

FIELD NOTES

THE GRA ━━━━ ON

Also by Teresa Jordan

Cowgirls:
Women of the American West

Riding the White Horse Home:
A Western Family Album

The Stories that Shape Us:
Contemporary Women Write about the West (co-editor)

Graining the Mare:
The Poetry of Ranch Women (editor)

FIELD NOTES FROM THE GRAND CANYON

Raging River, Quiet Mind

an illustrated journal

Teresa Jordan

with a Foreword by Ann H. Zwinger

Published in the United States by Johnson Books, a division of Johnson Publishing Company, 1880 South 57th Court, Boulder, Colorado 80301. E-mail: books@jpcolorado.com

9 8 7 6 5 4 3 2 1

"Sustenance" first published in *Writing Down the River: Into the Heart of the Grand Canyon*, photographed and produced by Kathleen Jo Ryan, Northland Publishing, 1998

Cover design by Debra B. Topping
Cover illustration by Teresa Jordan

Library of Congress Cataloging-in-Publication Data
Jordan, Teresa.
  Field notes from the Grand Canyon: raging river, quiet mind / Teresa Jordan.
  p.   cm.
  ISBN 1-55566-255-2 (alk. paper)
  1. Grand Canyon (Ariz.)—Description and travel. 2. Grand Canyon (Ariz.)—Pictorial
works. 3. Jordan, Teresa—Journeys—Arizona—Grand Canyon. I. Title.
F788.J67   2000
917.91′32—dc21   00-022170

Printed in the United States by
Johnson Printing
1880 South 57th Court
Boulder, Colorado 80301

For Hal,
my partner on the river of life

Foreword

*T*he Grand Canyon is intimidating before you even get there: the most gorgeous, the most visited, the most famous … and it's even worse when you arrive. There is little friendly about the formidable vistas from the South Rim, the often-brief experience most people have. Those who hike into the canyon ought to be aware that each footstep takes them back 20,000 to 30,000 years in time.

But the best way to register this magnificent place is on a river trip, the longer the better. The canyon's presence floods into your life down to the cell level. For many, a boat-trip down the 200-plus miles of canyon becomes an intense life-changing experience, with a huge challenge: how to make sense of, to truly understand, a landscape so vast and so stunning, and to perceive what is happening in their own psyches. Ay, there's the rub—how *do* you come to terms with this place?

For Theresa Jordan, understanding resides in the vibrant details: in the unnamed, unnameable colors that vibrate off the walls, or in the blessed greenness the river provides within a harsh desert, or the myriad changing hues in the water itself—peaking waves that reflect different colors on opposite sides, frothing white water that flares with undertones of emerald and sapphire. Although Jordan made this trip as a writer, the words turned out not to be enough and she added the music of color. Watercolors have been used over the centuries for just such field records. Even more appropriate here, watercolor partakes of the spirit of the river itself which becomes part of the medium and the message.

Field Notes from the Grand Canyon is an extraordinary field journal of an extraordinary journey, brushed and scribed by an extremely skilled and generous hand, through an observant eye, and an expressive, discerning intelligence. "Field notes" denotes the devoted observations of a naturalist, written on the spot, at the time, the paper polka-dotted with drops of water. It is not the more formal "journal" written with writing table, lamp, and pen, once removed. The charm of *Field Notes from*

the Grand Canyon is embedded in its intimacy, the sense that the note-keeper was not preparing this for publication but for connecting to a time and a place in a particular and personal way. The wise format echoes that sense of looking over Jordan's shoulder and following a mind and hand at work and, in so doing, receiving the gift of her awareness and her perceptions. This small book delivers a very large message: look and ye shall see. Be here now.

Field Notes from the Grand Canyon is the book to give to someone going down the Colorado River in the Grand Canyon for the first time—or the fiftieth. It is a field guide to how to understand a time and a place. May it send us all out for watercolors and paper to establish our own perspectives of the heart.

Ann H. Zwinger

Introduction

The night before my husband, Hal, and I put into the Colorado River at Lees Ferry to spend twelve days floating through the Grand Canyon, I couldn't sleep. I wasn't afraid, at least not of what I should have feared, the very real danger of the Colorado River and its rapids that rank among some of the most challenging in the world, especially during this year of record rainfall. No, the danger didn't scare me and in fact I hungered for it. Some years earlier I had spent a wild summer kayaking in Montana, and though that season comprised my entire white water experience, I knew the sheer adrenaline high that comes from close encounters of the death-defying kind, and I couldn't wait. By the end of the trip I would realize my hubris, and shudder at the complacency I brought to face the river's fury. But that knowledge was days and miles in front of me. This night before we set out, more mundane reasons kept me tossing and turning through the wee hours of the morning.

The truth was, both Hal and I had grown increasingly punchy as the trip approached. We were abandoning our daily obligations for two weeks, twelve days of which we would be completely beyond the reach of the news, out of touch with our offices, our fax machines, our voice mail, our e-mail. It seemed like an extravagance. It seemed impossible. How could we possibly leave our lives behind so carelessly and for so long?

To "leave our lives behind." To be "out of touch." The number of times such phrases slipped into our conversation as we focused on the trip ahead should have tipped us off to something.

We were nervous about other concerns as well. Earlier that night, our group had gathered for an orientation meeting: four professional guides, Todd, Dan, Andrew and Scott; two volunteer baggage boatmen, Phil and Mad Dog; and eighteen other guests like ourselves. The guides won our confidence immediately. They were young, athletic, and full of laughter, but they all had an edge as well, something

that made us believe they would react quickly and effectively in a crisis. The other guests seemed game, a varied group that included Keith, a Missouri farmer; Velentina, an Italian psychoanalyst; Bill, an electrician; Jack, an astronomer; and Lois, an accountant. I breathed a sigh of relief when we finished introducing ourselves; there didn't seem to be a ringer in the lot. But as the guides instructed us on safety and the rituals of meals, using the toilet, and setting and breaking up camp, both Hal and I realized how closely we would be living with these people. We're lone wolves, Hal and I, and we could feel the claws of claustrophobia closing in.

And then there was the sheer challenge of camping for such a long time. Both Hal and I had been avid backpackers in our younger days, but we had given in to the mantra of "too busy." Neither of us had done any serious camping for some time before we had gotten married six years earlier, and we had never camped with each other. What if one or both of us found we no longer had the heart for it? What if we turned into whiners? What if we saw something unlikable in each other that had mercifully escaped us before?

"This trip is about more than just sight-seeing." Dan's voice broke through my worries. "Most people find that the river changes their lives in some way. Sometimes that change is dramatic."

The impetus to go down the river had come in the form of an assignment. A few weeks earlier, photographer Kathleen Jo Ryan had asked if I would be one of fifteen women writers who contributed to a book she was producing in conjunction with the Grand Canyon Trust, *Writing Down the River: Into the Heart of the Grand Canyon*. I said yes immedi-

ately; whatever trepidation I felt on the eve of the adventure, I had dreamed of making just such a journey for years, ever since I first hiked the canyon in the late 1970s, right out of college.

A writer with an assignment always has to fight the urge to conceive the piece in advance of the actual experience. I'd like to think that I come to each new task without preconception, as a *tabula rasa* upon which deep truth can inscribe itself. In fact, I had a good idea that my piece would be about the power and grandeur of nature, and the need to reconnect with it. At the time, I had no idea how much I needed to reconnect with myself.

Our first afternoon on the river, the sky darkened and then exploded in cloudburst. We heard a roaring, first of thunder and then of something we couldn't name. Suddenly we were under attack as rocks and gravel and then boulders shot with artillery force out of the hundred waterfalls and cataracts that suddenly burst from the canyon's sheer walls. We huddled our rafts together in the middle of the river for safety, our terror laced with amazement at the power and beauty of it all. I have only to close my eyes to go back to the rawness of that moment and see us again, drenched to the bone and shivering, not so much from cold as from adrenaline. We were drunk on the smell of ozone and the taste of red dirt, and in that moment I knew that all my petty fears of the night before were senseless.

I had hiked the Grand Canyon. I had read everything I could get my hands on about it—from John Wesley Powell's accounts of his 1869 and 1872 expeditions, to geological studies to anthropological surveys to guide books. I expected the canyon to astonish me. It exceeded my wildest imaginings by at least a power of ten. That moment in the thunderstorm was an awakening of sorts, something I was to experience over and over in the next twelve days.

A recent *New York Times Magazine* article on sleep suggested that the human animal needs a good deal more of it than we get. Subjects who rested eighteen and twenty hours a day said they had never before felt more fully *awake*. On the river I realized that I needed a good deal less distraction than I had accepted as the daily pace of modern life. A new term has come into our language: polyphasia, the act of doing more than one thing at a time, as in talking to your travel agent while you drive the kids to work, or reading the paper while you peddle the exercise bike, or practicing Berlitz while you chop onions for spaghetti. On the river we did only one thing: we went down the river. It was as if each plunge through the 48-degree water of a rapid washed another layer of film off our eyes.

How do we make meaning out of the world that surrounds us? I suspect that many of us go along, day to day, making slight adjustments to what we already know, shaped by some overarching view of the world that we have formed, somewhat amorphously, through this process we call life. But every once in awhile, we find ourselves in the midst of something so grand that it knocks us off our pins.

The scale of the Grand Canyon is almost incomprehensible. It's not just the depth of its crevasse or the length of its run. No one can enter it without a humbling sense of its significance: you float down through hun-dreds of millions of years of the earth's history, surrounded by some of the oldest exposed rock in the world; you pass by billions and billions and billions of lives, remnant now in the limestone formed from unfathomable numbers of shells that sifted to the bottom of the prehistoric sea; you crash through rapids strong enough to literally carve the rocks around you, and miraculously you almost always emerge unscathed.

My parents tell me that I came out of the womb already babbling about something. However much they exaggerate, I was an intensely verbal child, now grown into an intensely verbal adult. I meet the world with language; it's how I understand things, how I make order out of chaos. But the Grand Canyon left me virtually speechless.

"The wonders of the place can not be adequately represented in symbols of speech, nor by speech itself," wrote John Wesley

Powell in 1869, confronted with a similar experience of awe. He turned to metaphors of music to help describe it, calling the canyon "a land of song where mountains of music swell in the rivers."

There is a Zen saying that when the student is ready, the teacher is there. Perhaps out of some instinct that I would need more than jottings in my journal, I had tucked a small set of watercolors into my bag at the last moment. But then I had carried the same set of watercolors on a dozen trips and had never brought them out: I was too self-conscious, too busy. On the river, that changed. I felt as if I couldn't get enough of the beauty around me; trying to sketch or paint was a way to step inside it. For the first time, I didn't care if the paintings were good or bad; I just wanted to look closely enough to make them. And since I had no way to capture the hugeness of the canyon, I found myself focusing on the smallest things, which suddenly, magically, began to hold the beauty of it all.

I had gone to the river hungry for adventure. I returned nourished in a hundred different ways. The essay that came out of that trip—titled "Sustenance" and included as the last chapter in this book—is, as I earlier anticipated, about the beauty and grandeur of nature, but in ways I had never imagined.

Of course we returned to our over-busy lives, to the phones and the faxes and the e-mail and the traffic. But the act of attention and the habit of the sketchbook have stayed with me. It might seem, after the grandeur of the Grand Canyon, that everything else would seem pale and disappointing. In fact, the opposite is true. Every day, if only for a few moments, I can step into the focus the sketchbook allows me, and I always emerge refilled with the beauty of what my eyes have landed on, no matter how small or insignificant it might at first appear. One of the guides told me that the river will give you what you most need to find, and this sketchbook was the river's gift to me. I offer it in turn in the hope that it will inspire you to find the river for yourself.

The Jump-off Point — Marble Canyon Lodge, August 31, 1997

We are confronted with how small the dry bags are, and how little we can take. My friend Judith tells me that no matter how little we take, we still won't use it all. But Right now, as we pare down our gear, I have to confront my fears. I'm not afraid of leaving civilization, time, or credit cards (in fact, in a Freudian slip of sorts, I left my wallet at home). But I realize I am afraid of being cold. I know the canyon can reach 120°. Still, the hardest thing to leave behind is my blue sweater, companion on so many adventures.

OUR MOTEL ROOM AT MARBLE CANYON IS FILLED WITH ALL THE STUFF WE BROUGHT THAT WE HAVE NO ROOM TO TAKE.

WE ARE LIVING
WITHIN THE
EMBRACE OF
SUCH WALLS.

CLOUDBURSTS TODAY IN THE
CANYON, & WATER EXPLODED
OFF THE RIM & OUT OF THE
WALLS. EERIE, TERRIFYING
ABSOLUTELY ASTONISHINGLY
BEAUTIFUL. I THINK I CAN
REMEMBER THE SMALLEST
CAMEO, BUT IT FAILS
COMPLETELY IN THE RENDERING.

WHILE The canyon was flashing (as
the guides call the state of flash
flood) so much silt was being
scoured from the canyon walls
that - in the middle of fierce
rain - we were caught in a dust
storm. When it was over, our
sunglasses were coated from
dust, & our eyes red from tearing

Another day of Rain and waterfalls and gloriously explosive thunder

upstream, a couple of miles before our camp, we played in a huge natural amphitheater, an overhang-cave that Powell estimated could seat 20,000. Tonight we camp under a much smaller overhang, + I hike to an even smaller secluded one

Lake: Keith told me that his memory is that Powell claimed the cavern could hold 50,000. In reality, it might hold 5,000. Even here, in this land of hyperbole, we humans exaggerate. Even super-human Powell is human in this way.

The view from the granaries at Nankoweep.

By noon on day four, it was so hot and sunny
that Hal and I found a shadowy grotto for lunch

D.A.Y 4

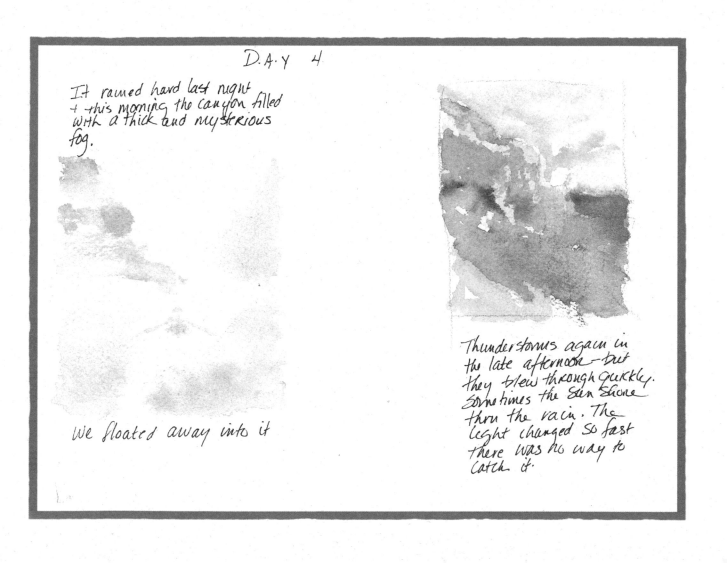

It rained hard last night
+ this morning the canyon filled
with a thick and mysterious
fog.

We floated away into it

Thunderstorms again in
the late afternoon — but
they blew through quickly.
Sometimes the sun shone
thru the rain. The
light changed so fast
there was no way to
catch it.

We woke this morning to clear skies. When the sun
popped over the Ridge, everything started steaming.
Early in the day's float, I looked upstream to see
a layering of unearthly blues, fading off into
the distance. A pathway, perhaps, to the heart's desire.

We have entered metamorphic Rock   granite, schist, + gneis.
We have dropped below the great unconformity, the missing
aeons. We are in ancient territory now. among some of the oldest
exposed rock on earth. The canyon is narrow and steep, the
rapids the wildest yet.

D·A·Y 5

WHAT COLOR IS the River
AT Dusk ?

ARRIVED AT PHANTOM RANCH TODAY ABOUT 10:00 A.M.
Dropped off 10 of our party and picked
up 12 new members. Hermit Rapids promptly
dumped several of the new ones into the Colorado.
Folks are good humored about it, and it looks like
we're in for a good trip

Colors have changed
entirely since we got
into the metamorphic
Rock. Right now I'm
simply dizzy with
them, unsure of
what I'm Really
seeing.

D·A·Y 6

We did 37 miles and a lifetime of rapids on this, the 2nd Day of terror, WITHOUT DUMPING ANYONE Out of a Boat. No, that's not quite true. Keith took an unexpected swim off the chuB, But · So far at least · he isn't talking about it.

ALSO, MAD DOG CRASHED THE Wall in Crystal and almost flipped, and TODD caught a life-defying wave in Spector.

A family of barrel cacti in the early morning sun...

Today we saw a large boulder of hornsblend schist. It's very orange, quite different than other rock we've seen. Dan was telling Todd he'd never seen a layer of it, only isolated boulders. A little later, he corrected himself. He started looking and had noticed a couple of layers here and there. How many things do we miss before we ask ourselves to look?

Our first full day of sun — glorious

D · A · Y   7

An amazing hike today, up the tapeats river to
its confluence with the Thunder River, then
up that to its source - a high waterfall bursting
out of the limestone. Then across Surprise
Valley with its blast furnace of radiating
boulders, and down Deer Creek to the
Throne Room, the Patio, and more
extraordinary oases. When we dove in
under the falls in the throne Room
you could almost hear our overheated
bodies sizzling

we walked through
a forest of prickly
pear, fully in bloom

The water in the pools under
the waterfalls was the
most extraordinary color

Keith told me what happened on the chub (baggage boat) yesterday. A wave in a rapid tossed the chub up on its side & threw him off. He surfaced & looked for the boat (the first rule when you hit the water is to find the boat) but he couldn't find it in the swells. A wave sucked him under. "It's so dark in a wave," he told me. "You have no idea how dark." He surfaced, still couldn't find the chub. A second wave sucked him down. Then he made the chub & was dragged to safety. "It's the first time I've been afraid of the river," he said. That's the difference between us tourists & the guides, I think — that the guides know enough to be afraid.

Keith is no longer a tourist...

Last night, Jack, the astronomer talked to us about the stars. He started with Newton's essential question — why is the night sky dark — and went on from there to give us a brief tour through astronomical theories to man's present day sense of the universe. It was a simple and eloquent talk, a fitting companion to this journey down the river thru geologic time — the earth's sense of itself

D·A·Y 8

We have been playing in the Muav limestone all day. We lunched at Matkatamiba, clamoring up a narrow split in the limestone to a vast patio — a lost paradise of terraces and pools and cool, shady overhangs. Tonight we camp at "The Ledges," layer after layer of limestone terraces overlooking the river. We will sleep near a ferry grotto — the site earlier of our first clear-water shower (without soap, of course) in days.

Today a zebra (king) snake
visited our camp
for breakfast

When I made a move to
get my camera, I scared
him and he disappeared
into a crack in the
limestone wall.

The agave or
century plant,
blooms once
every 20 years
or so.

They grow so tall
and straight that
Hal and I have
mistaken them
for telephone poles
up on the ridge

which gives me reason to depend, more and more,
on watercolor and memory

D·A·Y 9

We set camp late in the afternoon and a half moon
hovered gently above us in the pre-dusk sky.
A calm and welcoming spot — what we needed
since we were all drunk on adrenalin.
THIS WAS The day for Lava Falls — which we
reached about 4:30. The flooding had changed it, and
this, the wildest rapid on the river,
was more brutal than ever.

Todd made a perfect run, and
so did Dan and Phil. And then
mad dog got pushed
off to the side, dived
down a wave, and his
Raft spun as if caught
in the wash cycle.
He swam for safety, and we
fished gear out of the water for
the next couple of hours.
He was lucky to come thru safely.

Mad Dog got knocked off
his line and dove into
a hole as big as—
well, as big as the Grand Canyon.
When he knew the boat was
going to flip, he dove into the
waves. I remember seeing the boat
spit up out of the hole like a
squeezed watermelon seed. It stood
on its nose and all I could see was its
shiny black bottom. The rapid tore the frame from
the raft and popped two cylinders. Last night, by
lantern light, Todd and the crew repaired the rips—
four bronzed backs leaning intently over the slack yellow
rubber. It looked like either an ancient tribal rite
or a major surgical procedure and, in fact, it was both of those.

We have moved into basalt
country and camp at the
site of the old lava dam.

"The river," I overhear Todd say,
"is just the color I like my coffee."

D·A·Y   10

yesterday afternoon, a hot and parching wind
blew up canyon. but the morning dawned cool
+ moist... and didnt last long.

Yesterday I rode on the Chub with Phil and he gave me a quick synopsis of a couple of billion years of geologic history.

He pointed out that the basalt we see is actually the negative shape of the old River bed, which the lava filled. The River then cut a new course for itself thru the sedimentary Rock — an easier task than carving thru the impenetrable basalt.

We floated past the core of an ancient volcano.

limestone (calcium carbonate) is the Result of layer upon layer of seashells solidified under incredible pressure. "When I come down the River," Phil said, "I'm aware of rowing down thru billions and billions and billions of lives."

At the source of Thunder River we found fossilized snails in red sand.

D·A·Y 11

Morning comes to our little camp...

Another Quiet day on the River ...

We are back in metamorphic rock—Zoroaster granite, Vishnu schist, and gneiss—what Powell dreaded as the third granite gorge.

The granite often falls in sharp-edged blocks.

Vast walls are smooth and polished, sculpted, it seems, by Henry Moore.

D·A·Y 12

We packed our dry sacks for the last time this morning. For twelve days, everything we have needed or wanted has fit into these grocery-bag-sized black rubber containers. When we unpack them into our car in the parking lot at Pierce Ferry, we will be returning to a more material life, filled with things and diffusion.

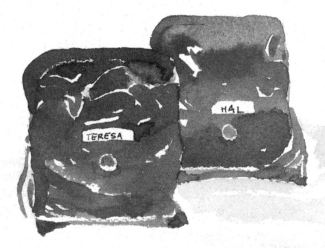

TERESA

HAL

When we left camp, we made a flotilla out of the rafts to float the hour to Separation canyon. Hal sang 'The Rivers of Texas,' Keith read to us out of his book, Frances sang "500 miles." The mood was somber, but very sweet.

People come on the river for so many reasons. Lois told me that, after her divorce two years ago, she'd learned to handle most parts of single life — bringing up her boys, running the household, making her living. But she was baffled by the idea of traveling alone. She figured a Grand Canyon trip would be so magnificent it wouldn't matter if no one else even talked to her. Besides, she told me, she'd just dropped her youngest child off at college; when she returned, it would be the first time she had ever lived alone. "How do you feel about it?" I asked her. "Excited," she answered. "Right now I feel like I can do anything."

For Hal and me, the question is — How do we keep this level of reverence and simplicity in our daily lives?

Sustenance

During the afternoon of our first day on the river, the world exploded. We were floating down Marble Canyon, a few miles below Lee's Ferry, when the clouds closed in. Thunder reverberated off the steep walls—a sound not like any thunder I had heard before, but a booming I might have expected in a siege of war, accompanied by flashes of blinding light. The clouds let loose gusting torrents of rain and suddenly the canyon seemed to blow apart as a hundred surging cataracts burst forth, great gushers of water that ran blood red with dirt and rock and boulders twice the size of cannonballs. Even as the needled rain burned our skin, we huddled in a dust storm, the air thick with grit, excoriated from 1200 feet of vertical fall. Such air has a texture like sandpaper, and when the rain let up enough we thought to look at one another, we saw that our eyes burned demon red.

Six guides accompanied us on our trip. Several of them had been down the Grand Canyon thirty times and more. Never, they all agreed, had any of them seen the canyon "flash" with such exquisite violence and beauty. Over the next twelve days I learned that each of them, on every trip, sees something he has never seen before.

My etymological dictionary tells me that the word "awe" comes from the Old Norse *agi*, akin to the Old High German *agison*, to frighten; from the Gothic words *agis*, fear, and *og*, I am afraid; from Old Irish *-agor*, I fear; and, more remotely, the Greek *akhors*, distress or pain. Our contemporary sense of the word retains some vestige of these origins; Webster's *New World Dictionary* defines awe as a mixed feeling of reverence, fear and wonder caused by something majestic or sublime. For twelve days and 280 miles on the river, I was filled with awe—so struck by it, in fact, that if I have any courage at all, I shall never be the same.

Overindulgence is a sin, but Aristotle thought it impossible to take in too much beauty. On the river, I found myself drunk with visual excitement, engaged in a gluttony of looking. Among the few possessions that I had stuffed into the grocery-bag-sized dry sack that carried my belongings, I packed a small box of watercolors, and I stole away from our group for a few moments each morning and afternoon to paint. Often I would try to recall something I had seen on the river. Other times I would focus on something directly in front of me: a family of barrel cacti in the late afternoon sun, a single cube of Zoroaster granite. On the rafts, I found myself looking with an engagement that made me blind to everything else, often forming a peephole with the crook of my little finger, trying to isolate, to understand, the purity of that particular gold of morning light on the ridge, or the muddy claret of the redwall limestone. Once, when I turned away from my own looking to take in my fellows, I realized that our boatman for the day, Scott, had set up his video equipment; Keith, a Missouri farmer, was taking notes for his book; Kathy, a Portland therapist, was photographing; and my husband, Hal, a radio producer, was recording the murmur of flat water and the roar of approaching rapids.

The children's author and artist Maurice Sendak once told an interviewer about his favorite piece of fan mail. A young boy had sent him a particularly charming drawing; Sendak sketched one of his "Wild Things" on a card and posted it back. A few weeks later, the boy's mother wrote that her son had loved the card so much he had eaten it. "That to me was one of the highest compliments I've ever received," Sendak told NPR's Terry Gross. "He didn't care that it was an original drawing. He saw it, he loved it, he ate it."

What feeds us, and what do we merely consume, insatiably hungry for more? As we floated off early one morning, I gazed upriver at receding lines of cliffs and talus slopes as they met the banks in the interlace of fingers in prayer. That evening, as I tried to recall the spectrum of blues—from the almost translu-cent cerulean of the slopes closest to me to the misty indigo of those farthest away—I yearned, with my tiny sketch, to ingest the blood and body of river and rock, not only to take it in, but to enter into it, to transcend, if only for a moment, the tissue that divides us from that which is not us, the mundane as much as the mystical and sublime.

I had climbed the steep hillside above our camp to paint, and when I finished I hiked down to join the easy conversation around *hors d'oeuvres* that had become the nightly habit of our group. That night, we talked about Princess Diana; her death had been the last news to reach us before we put in. The event had accompanied us these days on the river, a partner to the extraordinary beauty and power that swept us downstream, and now we wondered about the insatiable fascination that had hounded her literally to death, and our own part in it. Many of us were grateful for the remove the canyon gave us from the media orgy that we knew had erupted around the tragedy, and the titillated addiction we would have given into if we had access to the news. What did we—the world at large, and our own small selves—need from her, what hunger did we think she could satisfy? How full must we be before we cease to grab what glitters, just because it's there?

I asked myself this last question again a few days later when a small king snake crawled along a half-inch crag in the limestone behind our camp. We gathered to watch him and he grew perfectly still, aware of us but not, apparently, much disturbed. He was a beautiful thing, only two feet long, striped black and white with the precision of fine painted porcelain. I made a move for my camera and startled him. He jerked perceptively and then slithered away. I still wonder what I thought a photograph could capture that a longer moment of stillness would have failed to reveal.

Late in the afternoon of the eleventh day, shortly before we made camp for the last time, we stopped at Travertine Falls. We climbed a narrow slot in the limestone and shimmied up a sheer wall of gleaming black schist to reach a small travertine cathedral under a forty-foot waterfall, lit by a single shaft of sun. Each day on the river, embraced by such wonders, I had thought: this is the most magnificent sight I have ever seen. Surely, nothing can exceed this. A few miles later, the canyon would prove me wrong.

Our final morning, as I sat on my sleeping mat to sketch, I thought I would try to capture some essence of Travertine Falls. Instead, I found myself painting our black rubber dry bags: dark, amorphous shapes that nonetheless held, in the clarity of attention, a beauty as surprising as sunlight on schist. The bags were right in front of me; such mundane objects had been in front of me every day of my life. In awe, I realized I had never seen them, *really* seen them, before.

A river trip is a journey. If the current is strong, you don't go back, only farther along. On noon of the twelfth day, we reached Pierce Ferry, the end of our trip. We gathered with our river friends for one last meal, turkey sandwiches laid with dark green leaves of romaine and glistening jewels of cranberry sauce, and talked about how to hold onto the many gifts of the canyon. We talked, too, about the news that had greeted our landing, the death of Mother Teresa. After lunch, Hal and I packed our car to drive twelve hours straight home; Hal needed to catch a plane to New York in the morning.

Late that night, as the long yellow beams of our headlights cut across the black Nevada desert, I fell asleep and dreamt of gauzy white cotton backlit by sun, billowing under a deep azure sky. Just as I realized I was dreaming of India, I woke to hear Mother Teresa's funeral on the radio. The reception was poor and full of static; it drifted in and out and came from very far away, a dream itself perhaps, or a sacred invocation.

I reached out to my husband. "Are you okay?" I asked. "Do you want me to drive?"

"I'm fine," he answered. "I'm good." He squeezed my hand, then put his own back on the wheel. We drove on through the night toward the comforts of home, looking for the courage to change our lives.

Postscript

We hungered for the Grand Canyon from the minute we left it, and the following spring we planned a trip back, this time to experience the region from the South Rim. On our first trip, we were keenly aware that we were only visitors to this amazing place. Now, we wanted to meet people who called the Grand Canyon home. We met Kenton Grua, who had hiked the entire length of the canyon, over 500 miles when all the up-and-down is accounted for, the only known person to do so since the Anasazi Indians. We talked with Ross Knox who packs mules over 3500 miles a year, riding from rim to river and back again five days a week as he carries food into Phantom Ranch and garbage back out. Most of all, we wanted to visit Supai, the village home of the Havasupai tribe, who have lived along the fast blue waters of Havasupai Creek for over seven hundred years. The previous year, the creek had been in flood when we passed, and the villagers had been evacuated.

There are no roads into Supai. You can reach it by hiking five miles up from the river or eight miles down from the rim. You can also ride in on horse or mule. We opted for the most popular method among the Havasupai themselves: a ride in the tribal helicopter.

Here are a few pages from my second Grand Canyon journal.

We left home yesterday
morning and drove down
through Bryce and Zion
National Parks to
arrive late last night
at Jacob Lake Inn,
on the Kaibab Plateau near the
North Rim.

This morning I woke early
and went outside to explore...

I was simply
dazzled by the
pure orange bark
of the Ponderosas
in the early morning light.

The Desert View Watchtower is the highest point on the South Rim. It looks ancient but was actually built in 1932, the work of Mary Jane Colter, a contemporary of Frank Lloyd Wright's who drew inspiration from the remains of ancient canyon civilizations. As chief architect and designer for the Fred Harvey Company for over 40 years, she became the most celebrated woman architect of her day. She worked closely with Fred Kabotie, a young Hopi artist who went on to earn international fame.

Pictures of Colter show a small, fierce woman with unruly white hair.

The Hopis believe that they came into this world thru the Sipapu, a small hole in the heart of the Grand Canyon,

I wonder if the pull to emergence might have felt anything like what I felt as I stood on the main floor and looked up through the layers of balconies to the golden glow of the ceiling, lit by tall windows, just out of sight.

I've been reading Havasupai Legends by Smithson and Euler. Long, long ago, the steep walls of this canyon could open and close, crushing anyone foolish enough to venture in. But one day, two boys shot arrows at the walls when they started to close, and from that day on the canyon was safe for the Havasupai.

Another legend prophesies that the end of the tribe will come if the rock pinnacles ever tumble.

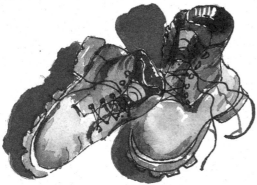

Introduced to the dust of Havasupai, Mary Beth's boots have lost that conspicuous newness.

It's mind boggling to think that everything in this canyon – with the exception of the rocks, the plants, and the river itself – had to get down here under its own steam, by pack train, or by airlift. It has given me a new appreciation for the accoutrements of Village life to think that every doorknob, every window, every sheet of corrugated tin or drywall or chainlink, every bathtub and mattress had to be somehow maneuvered down from the canyon rim into a world with no roads.

Today we witnessed the arrival of a refrigerator, stove, and washer and drier, each slung in a huge net & dangling below the 4-seater helicopter.

These fellows posed for me... until they had to go to work.

Last night, I stood outside for a long time waiting for the full moon to rise from behind the cliff. The barking of all the dogs in Havasupai echoed off the walls. Just when I thought the moon would never break free, a jet flew by, pulling a thread of moonlight across the sky.

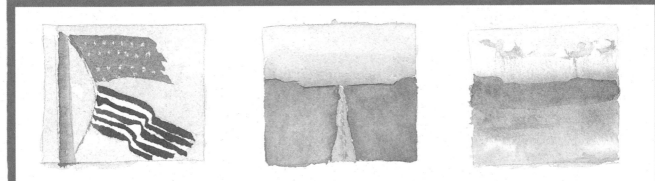

We headed home out of Flagstaff in a windstorm. On our way down, we'd noticed a huge, wind-tattered flag flying over the truck stop at Cameron, on the west edge of the Navajo Reservation. Today, when we passed back through, the wind had torn it in two. The air over the painted desert was filled with red earth. Thunderstorms chased us as we sped along the Vermillion Cliffs and even the clouds seemed heavy with dust.

The wind blew us home...

Acknowledgments

My heartfelt thanks to photographer Kathleen Jo Ryan who made possible my trip down the Grand Canyon through her invitation to contribute to *Writing Down the River,* and who first suggested I should seek publication for the sketchbook that came out of that journey. My immense gratitude also extends to our outfitter, Outdoors Unlimited, and the extraordinarily competent and caring group of young men who served as our guides and volunteer boatmen: Dan Hall, Todd Stanley, Scott Lindgren, Andrew Solomon, Samuel Philips and Matthew (Mad Dog) Maes. As for my fellow adventurers, I'd sign on to go down the river with every one of you again.

About the Author

Teresa Jordan and her husband, folklorist Hal Cannon, created the radio documentary series *The Open Road: Exploring America's Favorite Places*, featured on Public Radio International's *The Savvy Traveler*. Teresa is the author of the memoir *Riding the White Horse Home* and *Cowgirls: Women of the American West*, and has edited two anthologies of Western women's writing. She divides her time between a small ranch in northeast Nevada and a cabin in the mountains above Salt Lake City. You can visit her online at www.FieldnotesWest.com.

Ruby, the only labrador
in the known world
who is afraid of water

was glad to see us
return from the river
safely.